15 Simple Writing Tips

Top Tips From a Successful Full-Time Freelance Writer

INTRO

I'm not going to beat around the bush: writing full-time from home is hard work. But, I am going to provide you with 15 tried and true tips that will get your writing career rolling. Read through these tips and keep a copy of this tip book next to your bed or on your desk – quick tips and a bit of inspiration go a long way each day!

Have questions? Need some quick answers? Looking for some advice? Go ahead and contact me! You can find contact information on my website: www.hhalepis.com.

Now, it's time to start working your writing career!

TIP NUMBER ONE: Write What You Know.

The Sense Behind It: do you have a penchant for ballet? Know all about what it's like to be a single mom? Spend weeks working as an assistant chef? Spend some time thinking about the one thing (or maybe two things) that you really know about. You know, those things that you are passionate about? The things that make your world tick or that you do every day? Believe me, there's a market for what you know and what you can tell the world about what you know.

Simply Put: Find Your Niche.

TIP NUMBER TWO: Find Your Fingers.

The Sense Behind It: I know, you know where your fingers are, right? Your fingers are somewhere at the end of your palms and just past your knuckles, right? Writers know their fingers a bit different than everyone else. You see, our fingers ache and we know where all those aches come from – hours and hours of writing! Put your fingers to the test and get to know every inch of your print-padded digits.

Simply Put: Write As Much As Possible.

TIP NUMBER THREE: Become An Observer

The Sense Behind It: Hunter S. Thompson couldn't have written the Rum Diaries if he hadn't noticed some peculiar happenings in Puerto Rico. No matter where you go and no matter what you do, take note. See what's around you, but, more importantly, *feel* what's around you. Does the air have a certain smell? Did someone's smile or name stick with you? If you close your eyes and think back to an event, what do you hear? Learn to observe all that's around you.

Simply Put: Experience Life.

TIP NUMBER FOUR: Good Writers Read.

The Sense Behind It: Read everything from best sellers to the ads posted on subway cars. You can't be a writer if you don't read. Got an extra hour in your day? Pick up a book. See a free newspaper lying around? Pick it up and give it a read. Reading is the number one thing that great writers do and mediocre writers don't do enough of.

Simply Put: Read Like a Chef Eats.

TIP NUMBER FIVE: Learn To Take It

The Sense Behind It: You've got to have thick skin to be in this business. The poem that you love so dearly will be shot down. Your idea for the great work of fiction will be rejected. Editors will re-write your sentences and articles you spent hours working on will be sent back to you with lots of track changes edits. Don't bite back. Learn to take it.

Simply Put: Develop Crocodile Skin.

TIP NUMBER SIX: Realize Your Mistakes

The Sense Behind It: All writers have to deal with editors; it's just a fact. Some editors can provide truly excellent advice and these editors are worth their weight in gold. No matter who your editor happens to be, take the time to see what this person is trying to convey. You can always, always, always, learn from your mistakes and this will make you a stronger writer – forget the idea that you know it all, you don't.

Simply Put: Become a Know-Nothing

TIP NUMBER SEVEN: Don't Cut Out Content.

The Sense Behind It: When you start looking at forums and websites centered around writing, you'll see that a lot of people buck "content farms." Don't make this mistake. There are plenty of content companies on the Internet and many of them pay a fair wage. Even if payment per article seems low, you can always learn from the editors that you'll come across when working for a content company, and you can always double-up on the assignments that you take to make more cash. If you're just starting out, don't cut out content companies.

Simply Put: Content Companies Pay.

TIP NUMBER EIGHT: Use the Social Network Built for Business.

The Sense Behind It: there are lots of social networks out there. I'm sure you've already discovered the time-waster that Facebook is and how quickly you can learn about breaking news on Twitter, but have you given LinkedIn a try? In addition to setting up a LinkedIn account, make sure to sign up for some LinkedIn writing groups. Seasoned writers and editors from all walks of life take to the LinkedIn forums regularly to offer advice and to answer questions. Post some of your thoughts, find out what others things, and absorb all that you can from those who know.

Simply Put: Learn To Love LinkedIn.

TIP NUMBER NINE: Connect With Others.

The Sense Behind It: There are other people out there just like you. Those people are reading this book, learning to write, and building writing careers too. Connecting with those people will help you grow, find new gigs, and even form long-lasting partnerships. Find people who have the same plans that you do and forge friendships.

Simply Put: Collect Connections

TIP NUMBER TEN: Find Other Activities to Take Part In.

The Sense Behind It: Writing, dear readers, is a lonely profession. Writing for a living isn't all glamorous and you won't have lots of people to talk to day in and day out. Instead, it will be you and your computer (and maybe a cat or two). Trust me when I say that you'll want to participate in activities outside of writing – just remember to observe those activities whole-heartedly, so that you can go back to your cave (alright, office) and write.

Simply Put: One Is a Lonely Number.

TIP NUMBER ELEVEN: Join Job Lists

The Sense Behind It: I'm not talking about posting your resume on Monster or some other job board (not a bad idea, but little freelance work can be found this way). I'm talking about job lists that cater directly to writers and freelancers. To find these lists, just conduct a basic Internet search. You might have to shell out a few dollars per year to gain access to listings, but it's a heck of a lot easier than combing job sites each morning.

Simply Put: Let The Work Come To You.

TIP NUMBER TWELVE: Build a Basic Website.

The Sense Behind It: You don't need to hire a web designer to offer up a good website. WordPress sites will get the job done, just keep it simple. Your site should include a brief bio, short links to samples, contact information, and – most importantly – great content. Look over your site a hundred times, ask others to look at it, and make sure that it is not full of spelling, grammar, or other mistakes. This is a crucial step, since you'll be sending out a link to your website to all prospective clients.

Simply Put: Put Yourself Out There.

TIP NUMBER THIRTEEN: Do Some Free Work.

The Sense Behind It: I know, the notion of not getting paid is scary, but you'll need to provide new clients with samples and the best way to do that is to get your name in print. Since most publishers and website owners won't give you a byline if you don't have a portfolio, it's a great idea to find a site or a blog that will let you publish under your own name. If you get paid for the article you post, great! If not, swallow your pride and crank out a solid piece for free. You won't get paid, but you will have a sample of your work to show people.

Simply Put: Free Isn't Always Bad.

TIP NUMBER FOURTEEN: Don't Go Full-Time (Yet).

The Sense Behind It: At some point, you will be able to say "goodbye" to that cubicle, but not yet. It takes a long time to build up a roster of clients and a longer time to make decent wage writing. Spend some time getting your name out there and lining up a few clients before you settle down in your home office to work as a writer full-time. I know, it seems like a long road, but it will be worth it!

Simply Put: Don't Quit Your Day Job.

TIP NUMBER FIFTEEN: Don't Give Up!

The Sense Behind It: I'm putting on my fortune-teller cap for a moment. Here's what your writing career future holds: lots of rejection letters, grumpy editors, offers of coffee coupons instead of payment, chasing down money owed, and working weekends. Sounds fun, doesn't it? Well, writing can be a lot of fun and you can make money at it – but you can't let those rejections, grumpy editors, insulting offers, and sunny days spent inside get you down. Stick with it, write every day, send out tons of resumes, and never, never, give up hope. Once you get those clients, you'll be glad that you stuck with it!

Simply Put: Stick To Your Writing Career Like Glue!

Now That You're Off To A Good Start...

Here are some real examples from past and current clients that you might find useful (or just get a kick out of!).

On Writing What You Know

Example: I was once contracted to write about automotive engines. I spend quite a bit of time searching terms like "V6," "Boxster Engine," and "V4." I'll be honest, I live in the city so I don't drive very often. When I do drive, I simply step into my car, turn the key, and hope that I get where I need to go before I run out of gas. So, as you can imagine, my knowledge of automotive engines was limited (even after hours of researching) and it showed. I managed to write five pages of text and collect payment for the project, but I was never asked to expand on my car knowledge again!

On The Importance of Observation

Example: after spending quite a few hours on a train one time, I felt the need to jot down some words. Fingers quickly typing away, I came up with quite a few letters in a short span of time. Happy with my story, I asked my husband to read it once we got off the train in order to gain his feedback. He scrolled through the pages, snapped my laptop shut, and said, "The girl across from us was wearing striped tights? Strange, I sat across from her for four hours and I didn't notice that detail!" Writers always notice what's happening around them – that's how we turn mountains into molehills!

On Developing Thick Skin

Example: I've dealt with a lot of editors over the years (a stifling amount, really). Most of the editors I've had are great and I keep in touch with many of them. But, once in awhile, a really bad editor comes along. I equate poor editors to that old adage *"...those who can't teach, teach gym."* Some editors simply have chips on their shoulders and think (no, *know*) that they should really be writing what you're writing. One time, I came across a particularly bitter editor. After spending hours interviewing and researching, I submitted a contracted story to a popular magazine. The story was accepted and I awaited the final print.

The day that the issue was printed, I ran right out and purchase a copy. There it was: my story and my name printed under it! Only, I didn't recognize one single word. The entire story had been re-written from top to bottom. I wanted to cry, but instead I learned a good lesson instead. There are two kinds of editors: those who want you to shine and want to help you *and* those who just want to see things their way. I cherish the first kind and try my best to appease the later type.

On Connecting With Others

Example: Earlier in my career, I was lucky enough to connect with two other writers who I now talk with and gain insight from daily. At first, I was wary of reaching out to other writers for fear that we'd be competing against one another. Now, I really value what these other professionals offer me advice and communication-wise. Email and messenger programs are our form of a water cooler, and every writer needs other writers to bounce ideas off of.

On Building A Website

Example: I know, building a website seems like a lot of work. Believe me, though, you really need that website if you are going to write full-time as a freelancer. At the start of my career, I didn't have a website with my own URL. This was a big mistake. I often directed prospective clients to my blog, which really consisted of short stories (not what top-paying clients want to see). Later, I built a website, paid for hosting, and gained my own URL. Now, I direct clients to my own website that features my portfolio and some of my samples. This site makes my professional life a heck of a lot easier!

On Writing For Free

Example: every writer out there will tell you not to write for free. I disagree. If you are just starting out, there are some very good websites and blogs that will post your work (with credit), but not for a paid fee. My very first gig was submitting a recipe to a blog for moms. I'm wasn't a mom, I didn't know anything about mothering, but I did know how to write and cook. That blog post I wrote only took me a few minutes to create, but I was able to share it with friends, family members, and, most importantly, prospective clients. I'm not telling you to write for free all the time, but sometimes it just pays off in other ways.

A Brief Note About My Next Book

Like what you've read here? Make sure to stay tuned for my next tip book: *"15 Ways To Keep Your Writing Career Rolling!"* I'll cover all that you need to know about keeping your clients happy and maintaining customers who really matter.

www.ingramcontent.com/pod-product-compliance
Lightning Source LLC
Chambersburg PA
CBHW072031190526
45166CB00015B/1791